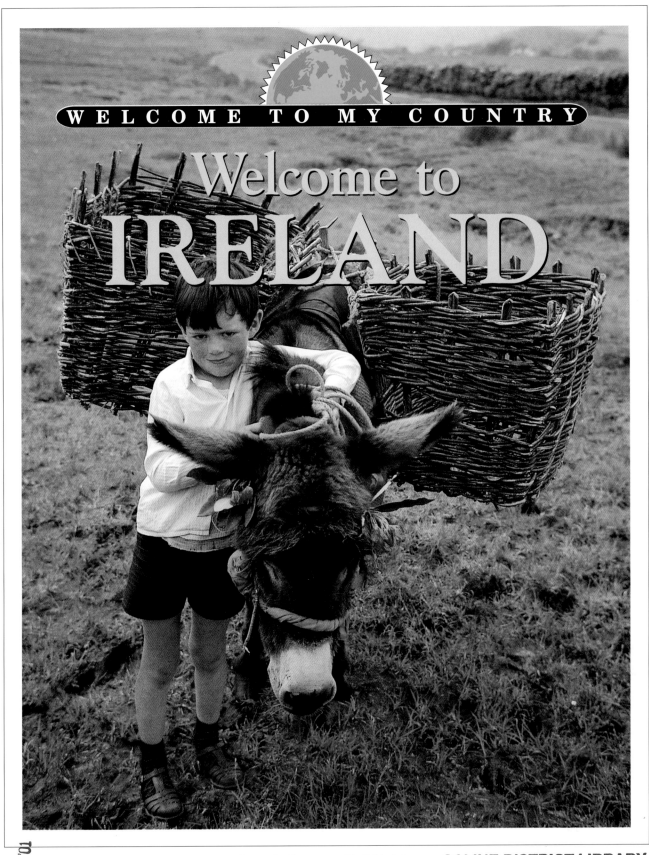

WELCOME TO MY COUNTRY

Welcome to
IRELAND

Gareth Stevens Publishing
A WORLD ALMANAC EDUCATION GROUP COMPANY

Written by
DORA YIP/SHANNON SPENCER

Designed by
JAILANI BASARI

Picture research by
SUSAN JANE MANUEL

First published in North America in 2001 by
Gareth Stevens Publishing
A World Almanac Education Group Company
330 West Olive Street, Suite 100
Milwaukee, Wisconsin 53212 USA

For a free color catalog describing
Gareth Stevens' list of high-quality books
and multimedia programs, call
1-800-542-2595 (USA) or
1-800-461-9120 (CANADA).
Gareth Stevens Publishing's
Fax: (414) 332-3567.

© **TIMES EDITIONS PTE LTD 2001**
Originated and designed by
Times Editions
An imprint of Times Media Private Limited
A member of the Times Publishing Group
Times Centre, 1 New Industrial Road
Singapore 536196
http://www.timesone.com.sg/te

Library of Congress Cataloging-in-Publication Data
Yip, Dora.
Welcome to Ireland / Dora Yip and Shannon Spencer.
p. cm. -- (Welcome to my country)
Includes bibliographical references and index.
ISBN 0-8368-2518-7 (lib. bdg.)
1. Ireland--Juvenile literature. [1. Ireland.]
I. Spencer, Shannon. II. Title. III. Series.
DA906 .Y66   2001
941.5--dc21   00-057352

Printed in Malaysia

1 2 3 4 5 6 7 8 9 05 04 03 02 01

PICTURE CREDITS
A.N.A. Press Agency: 3 (center), 9 (top), 36
Archive Photos: 15 (top), 15 (center), 16,
    29 (bottom, left)
Bes Stock: 43
Holzbachova Benet: 4, 11, 13, 24, 26, 33,
    35, 37, 39
Michele Burgess: 41
Jan Butchofsky: 34
Focus Team: 3 (bottom), 20, 25, 27, 28, 30,
    38, 40 (both)
Blaine Harrington: 19, 29 (top),
    32 (bottom), 45
HBL Network: 14
Ingrid Horstman: 22
Dave G. Houser: 10
The Hutchison Library: 7, 17, 18
International Photobank: 2, 6
Topham Picturepoint: cover, 1, 12, 15
    (bottom), 21, 29 (bottom, right), 31,
    32 (top)
Trip Photographic Library: 3 (top), 8,
    9 (bottom), 23

Digital Scanning by Superskill Graphics Pte Ltd

Contents

Words that appear in the glossary are printed in **boldface** type the first time they occur in the text.

Welcome to Ireland!

Covered with brilliant green grass, Ireland is also called the Emerald Isle. The Republic of Ireland, where most of the people are Catholic, shares the island with Northern Ireland, which is part of the United Kingdom. The history of Ireland has been colorful, filled with clashes between different groups. Today, Ireland is mainly peaceful — a nation with warm, friendly people who love music and storytelling.

Opposite: People from all over the world visit the Blarney Stone, which is believed to magically make people great storytellers. The Stone is in the ruins of Blarney Castle, built in 1446.

Flag of the Republic of Ireland

Also called the Irish tricolor, the flag has been in use since the Easter Rising of 1916. The green band represents the Irish Catholics, and the orange band symbolizes the British Protestants. The white band stands for peace.

Flag of Northern Ireland

Adopted in 1953, this flag is based on England's flag. The red cross represents Saint George, England's patron saint. The six-pointed star is for the six counties of Northern Ireland, which officially shares the flag of the United Kingdom.

The Land

Lying west of Great Britain, the island of Ireland is small, measuring 32,588 square miles (84,403 square kilometers). Its landscape varies from rugged cliffs to rolling hills and wetlands. Much of the countryside is covered by pasture, which is used mainly for farming and grazing.

The Blue Stack Mountains in County Donegal and the Caha Mountains in

Below: Ireland's beautiful scenery is often reflected in the writing and art of its people. This picture shows Bantry Bay in County Cork.

Counties Kerry and Cork form Ireland's main mountain ranges. The longest river in Ireland is the River Shannon.

Dublin

Dublin is the capital of the Republic of Ireland. Some of its most important buildings line the banks of the River Liffey, which runs through the center of the city.

Seasons

Ireland has a cool climate with four seasons. Temperatures range from about 60° Fahrenheit (16° Celsius) in summer to 43° F (6° C) in winter. The mountains have harsher winters.

Rainfall averages about 2 inches (51 millimeters) per month during spring and summer. During autumn and winter, rainfall averages 3 inches (76 mm) per month. Western Ireland is the wettest region on the island. So much rain keeps Ireland emerald green.

Above: Due to the temperate climate and the abundance of rain, Ireland's landscape has lush green grass all year round.

Plants and Animals

The very wet climate of Ireland's western coast gives it the greatest variety of plant life in the country. It is home to the grass-like thrift, Kerry lily, and sundew plants. It is also a prime location for bird-watching.

Snakes do not exist on the island. Legends say that Saint Patrick, the patron saint of Ireland, drove them out. Gray seals feeding off the Atlantic coast and otters, or "river dogs," swimming in shallow waters off rocky coasts are common sights in Ireland.

Above: One famous bird that nests on Ireland's largely undeveloped western coast is the puffin.

Left: Alpine goldenrod adds color to the barren landscape of the Burren, a limestone plateau in the western part of Ireland.

History

The **Celts** (KELTZ), also known as the *Gaels* (GAYLZ), came from the European mainland and invaded Ireland around the sixth century B.C. They defeated the Firbolg, a native Irish people about whom little is known. Although Ireland was invaded by many other groups of people in the following centuries, it held on to many of its Celtic traditions.

Below: Gallarus Oratory is one of the oldest churches in Ireland. It was built some time between the sixth and ninth centuries.

English Rule

When King Henry II of England claimed Ireland in the twelfth century, he started a clash between English laws and **Gaelic** (GAY-lik) traditions. Gaelic society was made up of different tribes who shared common laws and customs. When the English leaders arrived, they removed this tribal system and introduced new laws. Later, England's King Henry VIII brought a new religion to the Catholics in Ireland — the Protestant religion.

Above: Thomas Fitzgerald, a Catholic **clan** leader, rebelled against King Henry VIII in 1534. Along with most Irish Catholics, he was furious when King Henry created the Church of England and made it England's official religion. Fitzgerald was executed in 1537.

Left: Civil wars between Protestant and Catholic militant groups began in Northern Ireland after the Easter Rising of 1916.

Penal Laws

The Catholic Irish were unhappy about losing their Gaelic customs and tried to rebel against the English. The English stopped further uprisings by introducing the **Penal Laws**, which stripped the Catholics of most of their rights. These laws were lifted in 1791 and 1829.

Political Change

In 1905, Arthur Griffith formed Sinn Fein, an Irish Catholic group that is still influential. In 1916, Sinn Fein was linked to the Easter Rising, a failed rebellion against British rule. But Sinn

Fein won most of the Irish seats in the British parliamentary elections of 1918.

Sinn Fein leader, Eamon de Valera, refused to sit in England's Parliament. He declared Ireland a republic. When the British outlawed Sinn Fein, the Irish formed the Irish Republican Army (IRA) to oppose British rule and fight for recognition of the Irish republic.

In 1920, Ulster (Northern Ireland) and Catholic Ireland (southern Ireland) officially separated. De Valera became the Irish prime minister in 1932 and established the sovereign nation of Ireland, or Eire.

Below: The ministers of the **Dail Eireann** (Irish Assembly) met a British peace delegation in 1921. The Dail rejected the British home rule bill of 1920, which established two separate parliaments for north and south. Southern Ireland became the Irish Free State in 1922.

The Republic of Ireland

Eamon de Valera formed the Republic of Ireland on April 18, 1949, separating the country from Britain and reclaiming Northern Ireland. No response was made to this claim until the late 1960s, when fights broke out between the Protestants and Catholics in Northern Ireland. Although many peace agreements have been made, this fighting has continued over the decades. The most recent peace accord, the 1998 Good Friday Peace Agreement, is still in force.

Left: Supporters surround Gerry Adams, the leader of Sinn Fein.

Daniel O'Connell (1775–1847)

Also known as "the liberator," Daniel O'Connell led the fight for Catholic freedom from British rule. He worked to end **compulsory** support for the Protestant Church of Ireland. In 1841, he became the first Catholic Lord Mayor of Dublin since the thirteenth century.

Daniel O'Connell

Eamon de Valera (1882–1975)

American-born Eamon de Valera took part in the Easter Rising of 1916 and was elected president of Sinn Fein in 1917. He became president of the Republic of Ireland in 1959.

Eamon de Valera

Mary Robinson (1944–)

Elected president in 1990, Mary Robinson used the position to focus attention on social issues. Because she is a Catholic, her marriage to a Protestant provided a new-style role model for the people of Ireland.

Mary Robinson

Government and the Economy

The Republic of Ireland is a representative democracy. The Parliament has two chambers. The Dail Eireann has 166 members, all of whom are elected by the public. The **Seanad Eireann** is made up of sixty members who are either appointed or elected.

Left: In 1998, Irish president Mary McAleese addressed the issues of freedom of speech and victims' rights at Harvard University in the United States.

The prime minister is the most powerful person in the Irish government. Nominated by the Dail, the candidate is then appointed by the president. The present prime minister, or *Taoiseach* (TEE-shock), is Bertie Ahern.

The Irish president guards the **constitution**, signs bills into law, and has the right to address both houses of Parliament. The current Irish president is Mary McAleese.

Economy

Since the 1970s, the Irish economy has undergone many changes. "The troubles" (the period of political struggle between Catholics and Protestants) has slowed down growth in Northern Ireland. In the Republic, however, tax **incentives** have attracted foreign business and money.

Agriculture

Fishing and agriculture, especially cattle ranching, are very important to

Below: Farming is still important in Ireland.

the Irish economy. Tourism is also a growing industry. More than three million people visit the Republic every year. However, Irish soil is stony, and farmers find it hard to make a profit from it.

Traveling in Ireland
Ireland's excellent transportation system provides bus services to even the most unpopulated areas of the island. The railroad also serves the entire country.

People and Lifestyle

Most Irish people can trace their roots back to the early northern Europeans who lived on and near the island. In the nineteenth century, many Irish left for countries like England, Canada, and the United States as a result of the Great **Famine** of 1845–1848. At present, about half of the Republic's population is under the age of twenty-five.

Irish people who live in cities tend to have modern lifestyles. They work in

Left: Many Irish have the light skin and hair of northern peoples.

Left: Known as the Gypsies of Ireland, the Travellers are a band of people who live by roadsides and carry all their possessions along with them. Like the traditional Gypsies, they roam the countryside.

offices, ride the train to work, and often end the day at a pub, where they visit with friends.

The rural Irish, such as farmers, tend to have more traditional lifestyles. They start their days early because they have to do chores and look after the animals. They often socialize with friends in the evening.

Family Life

Irish families are often tightly knit. Children are included in most adult gatherings, such as concerts and dance performances.

Attracted by opportunities abroad, many young Irish travel to other countries to work. Although some of them return to Ireland and use the skills they have learned, many end up staying in their **adopted** homelands. Popular destinations include the United States and Canada.

Above: Irish weddings are ideal opportunities for families and friends to get together.

Many Irish houses are traditional single-story cottages made of stone and plaster. However, a few people choose to live in high-rise apartments because they are less expensive.

Left: Very few high-rise apartments are built in Ireland because many Irish people like to live in a house with land.

Education

Most of the Irish population is well-educated. The state partly pays for and supervises the public schools, but they have usually been run by the Catholic Church, the Protestant Church, or other local organizations. Today, this religious **dominance** is decreasing as teachers and administrators are less tied to the Church.

Below: Day trips organized by schools or other organizations are very common in Ireland. Here, a group of girls is visiting Bantry House near Cork.

Irish students study history, English, mathematics, Gaelic, foreign languages, and other subjects. In their free time, students participate in **extracurricular** activities, such as music, riding lessons, and Irish step dancing. Other popular pastimes include singing and playing sports.

The government funds higher education, so many Irish citizens are able to earn college degrees. The Republic's most **prestigious** institution is Trinity College in Dublin.

Above: Trinity College in Dublin has educated some of Ireland's most famous scholars.

Religion

About 90 percent of the people in the Republic of Ireland are Catholic. In Northern Ireland, most of the population is Protestant. Although the Protestants and Catholics have clashed in Northern Ireland, they live peacefully side-by-side in the Republic. This is mainly because the Republic is so solidly independent.

The Catholic Church in the Irish Republic runs most of the schools, as well as some hospitals.

Left: A group of Catholic altar boys is part of a festival procession in County Cork.

Left: Built in the twelfth century, the Protestant Christ Church Cathedral in Dublin stands on the site of an eleventh-century Viking church.

Dublin, the capital of the Irish Republic, is home to many different religious groups. Minority religions include Judaism and Islam. Folk religions are not as common as in the past. Today, most folk beliefs and stories are regarded as legends.

Language

Gaelic and English are the official languages of Ireland. About 11 percent of Ireland's people speak Gaelic fluently. All students must learn the language, and government workers are required to be familiar with it as well.

Above: The ninth-century Book of Kells is one of the many manuscripts and books that is housed in the Long Room of the Old Library at Dublin's Trinity College.

When pronouncing Gaelic words, emphasis is usually placed on the first syllable of every word. The Irish alphabet has eighteen letters. It is made up of thirteen consonants and five vowels.

Storytelling is a very important part of Irish culture. Tales are based on folk legends or famous historical events.

Ireland has produced some of the world's greatest writers. Irishman James Joyce wrote famous books. Well-known Irish **playwrights** include Oscar Wilde and Samuel Beckett. William Butler Yeats and Seamus Heaney are among Ireland's finest poets.

Above: A road sign shows the names of towns in both English and Gaelic.

Below: Poet W. B. Yeats (*below, left*) and playwright George Bernard Shaw (*below, right*) are among the greatest Irish literary figures.

Arts

Ireland is a country filled with music and dancing. Traditional instruments, such as the button accordion, *uillean* (IL-awn) pipes (similar to the bagpipes), harp, tin whistle, fiddle, and *bodhran* (BOAR-an), give Irish music its distinctive **lilt**. Singing often accompanies the music.

Dancing

Traditional Irish step dancing has become popular in recent years. In

Left: Buskers, or street performers, are a common sight on the streets of major towns throughout Ireland.

Left: Although most step dancers are girls or women, boys and men are becoming increasingly interested in this traditional dance.

some rural areas, Sunday village dances are events that everyone looks forward to. These dances, called *ceilis* (KAY-lees), mix traditional dancing and music.

Step dancing is performed with the legs and feet — the dancers' arms rarely move. The dancers wear ballet-type shoes and costumes with beautiful Gaelic designs.

Architecture

Many of Ireland's buildings have been damaged throughout its long and often violent history. In the mid-seventeenth century, English armies destroyed castles, monasteries, and towns as England tried to control Ireland. Numerous architectural sites have survived, including prehistoric passage tombs, Iron Age ring forts, and stone round towers. Irish homes range from thatched-roof cottages to grand nineteenth-century mansions.

Above: Many of Ireland's impressive architectural sites, such as Dromoland Castle in County Galway, are open to the public.

Below: This entrance is an early twentieth-century Georgian doorway.

Traditional Crafts

The tourist trade has helped revive traditional Irish crafts. Textiles are among the most traditional Irish crafts. They include woolen clothing, Irish linen products, and handmade Irish lace. Jewelry-making is also a traditional craft. Designs are usually based on Celtic patterns and myths or on local plants and wildlife. The most common piece of jewelry is probably the Claddagh **betrothal** ring. Other craftspeople make pottery, musical instruments, and fine glassware.

Left: Irish actor Liam Neeson plays the title role in *Michael Collins*, a film about a famous revolutionary leader of the IRA.

Leisure

The Irish are very sociable people. They enjoy getting together with family and friends, and they love music and storytelling. Playing traditional instruments and composing songs is as popular as watching television or listening to the radio. The Irish also love outdoor activities, such as walking in the countryside, going boating, or playing Gaelic football.

Below: Residents of Lismore in County Waterford sit and watch the world go by.

GAA Clubs

The Gaelic Athletic Association (GAA), which was founded in 1884 and is funded by the state, promotes traditional Irish sports. Today, it has over 800,000 members. GAA clubs sponsor sports and social centers.

The Irish Pub

Irish pubs are very popular places to spend a relaxing evening. People go to pubs with family and friends for meals or drinks.

Sports

Gaelic football is one of the most well-loved traditional Irish games. It is similar to soccer and rugby in that it is played with a ball on a field. Gaelic football fever breaks out all over Ireland during the All-Ireland finals held in Dublin.

Hurling, a fast-paced field sport, is also very popular among the Irish. Players move the ball with sticks that look like those used in hockey. Girls and women play camogie, which is similar to hurling.

Other sports the Irish enjoy include soccer, rugby, golf, darts, horse racing, and fishing.

One of the most famous Irish sports figures is cyclist Sean Kelly, who won the Tour of Spain in 1988 and the Tour of Switzerland in 1990. He learned to cycle on Ireland's small country roads and eventually got the nickname "Man for All Seasons." In 1989, Kelly was named European of the Year, and his hometown named a square after him.

Left: The Irish Derby attracts a wide range of supporters. Many of Europe's best horses and horse owners participate in this racing event.

Festivals

Saint Patrick's Day is probably the most widely celebrated religious festival in Ireland. It **commemorates** the famous saint who is said to have driven out all the snakes from Ireland.

Below: Traditional music played by bagpipe bands fills the streets on Saint Patrick's Day on March 17.

Ireland also hosts many music festivals, such as the Adare Jazz Festival and the Ballyshannon International Folk Festival. Other festivals, such as the Galway Festival, focus on the arts and traditional culture.

The Kilkenny Arts Festival, held for ten days in mid-August, is probably Ireland's top arts festival. It features the work of local craftspeople and artists, and includes classical music, crafts, movies, poetry, and drama.

Below: Rows of spectators line the streets to watch performers in a Children's Day parade.

The Lisdoonvarna Matchmaking Festival is a fun event that spans the month of September and the first week of October. People gather in the pubs to sing and dance, and to keep an eye out for potential husbands or wives!

Food

Left: A favorite Irish dish is roast lamb with mint jelly or sauce.

A traditional Irish breakfast consists of fried eggs, bacon, sausages, grilled tomatoes, and bread. Farmers ate this big breakfast, called a "fry," to help them do the hard work on their farms. Dinner, served at noon, was the main meal. "Tea," a lighter meal, was served at the end of the day.

As the lifestyles of many Irish have changed, so have their eating habits.

Below: Irish coffee, a mixture of coffee, cream, and whiskey, is a popular drink among the Irish.

Today, breakfast and midday meals are usually lighter. Larger meals are eaten at the end of the working day, when family members can eat together. However, the traditional Irish fry is still served in hotels and inns.

Favorite foods include lamb, fresh fish, local cheeses, and scones (biscuit-like bread). Shops called "chippers" sell fish and chips (French fries).

Below: This couple is enjoying a meal at a medieval banquet.

IRELAND

Above: These brightly-painted fishing boats have been moored for the day.

Atlantic Ocean
A1–A5

Bantry Bay B5
Belfast (N. Ireland)
D2
Blarney B4
Blue Stack
Mountains C1

Caha Mountains
A5–B5
Carlow, county C4
Carrantuohill B4
Cavan, county C2
Celtic Sea B5
Clare, county B3–B4
Cork, city B4
Cork, county B4–B5
Croagh Patrick B3

Donegal, county C1
Dublin, city D3
Dublin, county D3

Galway, county B3

Irish Sea D3–D4

Kerry, county
A4–B4
Kildare, county
C3–D3
Kilkenny, country
C4

Laois, county C3
Leitrim, county C2
Liffey, River D3
Limerick, county B4
Lismore C4
Longford, county
C2–C3
Lough Neagh
(N. Ireland) D2
Lough Ree C3
Louth, county D2

Mayo, county
B2–B3

Meath, county
C3–D3
Monaghan, county
C2

North Channel D1
Northern Ireland
C1–D2

Offaly, county C3

Roscommon,
county B2–C3

Scotland D1

Shannon, River
B4–C2
Sligo, county B2

Tipperary, county
C3–C4

Ulster (N. Ireland)
C1-D2

Waterford,
county C4
Westmeath,
county C3
Wexford, county D4
Wicklow, county D3

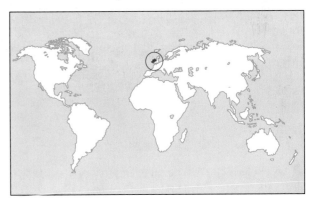

Quick Facts

Official Name The Republic of Ireland (Northern Ireland and Great Britain together make up the United Kingdom)

Capital Dublin (Northern Ireland's capital is Belfast)

Official Languages English and Gaelic

Population 3,632,944 (Republic); 1,663,300 (N. Ireland)

Land Area 27,136 square miles (70,282 square km)

Counties Carlow, Cavan, Clare, Cork, Donegal, Dublin, Galway, Kerry, Kildare, Kilkenny, Laois, Leitrim, Limerick, Longford, Louth, Mayo, Meath, Monaghan, Offaly, Roscommon, Sligo, Tipperary, Waterford, Westmeath, Wexford, Wicklow

Main Rivers River Liffey, River Shannon

Main Religion Catholicism (Northern Ireland is mainly Protestant)

Currency Punt, or Irish pound
(IR£0.87 = U.S. $1 in 2000)

Northern Ireland uses the pound sterling
(£0.64 = U.S. $1 in 2000)

Opposite: Ivy and colorful flowers cover many Irish homes.

Glossary

adopted: taken as one's own.

bodhran (BOAR-an)**:** a round, hand-held drum that makes a soft thump when it is struck with a short wooden drumstick, or beater.

betrothal: an engagement; a promise to marry.

ceilis (KAY-lees)**:** a form of traditional Irish entertainment that combines dancing and music.

Celts (KELTZ)**:** members of a group of western European peoples, including the ancient inhabitants of Britain and Gaul (France) and their descendants, especially in Ireland, Wales, Scotland, and parts of England.

clan: tribe or family group.

commemorates: serves as a memorial or reminder of something.

compulsory: must be done; required.

constitution: the principles by which a state is organized.

Dail Eireann: the Irish Assembly, which consists of 166 elected members.

dominance: a controlling influence.

extracurricular: outside the regular program of school classes.

famine: great hunger; extreme and widespread lack of food.

Gaelic (GAY-lik)**:** relating to Celtic history and culture; a Celtic language spoken in Ireland and Scotland.

incentives: things that encourage a person to do something; payments.

lilt: a way of speaking in which a person's voice rises and falls in a pleasant, musical way.

Penal Laws: a set of laws imposed on Catholics in the seventeenth and eighteenth centuries by Protestants in Britain and Ireland. These laws removed social and economic rights from Catholics, including the right to own or lease land, to vote, or to ordain new priests.

playwrights: people who write plays.

prestigious: having a good reputation.

Seanad Eireann: the Irish senate, consisting of sixty members who are either appointed or elected.

Taoiseach (TEE-shock)**:** prime minister of the Republic of Ireland.

uillean (IL-awn) **pipes:** a traditional Irish instrument similar to bagpipes.

More Books to Read

Allyn's Embarrassing and Mysterious Irish Adventures. Carol McGinley. (AGA Publishing)

And God Blessed the Irish: The Story of Patrick. Chris Driscoll (Ambassador Books)

Dublin. Cities of the World series. Deborah Kent (Children's Press)

The Easter Rising. Richard Killeen (Raintree Steck-Vaughn)

Everything Irish. Annmarie O'Grady (O'Brien Press)

Irish Folkstories for Children. Edmund T. Leamy and T. Crofton Croker (Irish American Book Company)

Ireland. Festivals of the World series. Patricia McKay (Gareth Stevens)

Katie's War: A Story of the Irish Civil War. Aubrey Flegg (O'Brien Press)

Videos

Amazing Wonders of the World — Wondrous Kingdom: England, Scotland and Ireland. (Questar)

Going Places: Ireland. (Mpi Home Video)

Legends of Ireland: Saint Patrick/ Brendan the Navigator. (Acorn Media)

Today — Journey Back to Ireland. (New Video Group)

Web Sites

www.ireland.travel.ie/home/index.asp

www.catholic.org/saints/patrick.html

www.gallica.co.uk/contents.htm

www.gaa.ie/sports/hurling/index.html

Due to the dynamic nature of the Internet, some web sites stay current longer than others. To find additional web sites, use a reliable search engine with one or more of the following keywords to help you locate information about Ireland. Keywords: *Belfast, Dublin, Gaelic football, Irish, River Shannon, Saint Patrick.*

Index